# THE
# DAM BUSTERS

## Martin W. Bowman

AMBERLEY

First published 2009
Amberley Publishing Plc
Cirencester Road, Chalford,
Stroud, Gloucestershire, GL6 8PE

www.amberley-books.com

Copyright © Martin W. Bowman, 2009

ISBN 978 1 84868 381 9

The right of Martin W. Bowman to be identified as the
Author of this work has been asserted in accordance
with the Copyrights, Designs and Patents Act 1988.

British Library Cataloguing in Publication Data.
A catalogue record for this book is available from the
British Library.

Typesetting and Origination by FONTHILL MEDIA.
Printed in Great Britain.

# CONTENTS

# INTRODUCTION

Perhaps the most famous RAF Squadron currently flying, 617 Squadron was formed at RAF Scampton on 21 March 1943 and equipped with Avro Lancasters specifically to undertake Operation *Chastise*, the breaching of dams vital to the German war effort.

The Lancaster evolved from the twin-engined Avro Manchester, which was one of several heavy bombers in the planning stages as the war began in 1939. The prototype Manchester flew in 1939 but was plagued by instability and problems with its complex, 24-cylinder Rolls-Royce Vulture engines. Of the 202 Manchesters built more were lost to engine failure than enemy action, but the aircraft's designer, Roy Chadwick, had made plans to add 12ft to the wingspan and replace the two troublesome Vulture engines with four Rolls-Royce Merlin V-12s and the result was the Lancaster, which flew for the first time in January 1941. Large production orders were placed and soon Avro's production facilities were overwhelmed and numerous other companies and contractors joined the effort to produce Lancasters. Consisting of 55,000 separate parts, it has been estimated that half a million different manufacturing operations were involved to produce just one aircraft. Peak production was achieved during August 1944 when 293 aircraft were built.

Lancasters first flew operationally in March 1942. A pilot, flight engineer, navigator, wireless operator and bomb aimer/front gunner completed the crew of seven. It was regarded as 'a pilot's aeroplane'

which inspired confidence. The 'Lanc' became the most successful bomber operated by the RAF and the Royal Canadian Air Force. The aircraft had speed and lifting power that no other aircraft of the day could match.

Weighing 36,900lb empty, the Lancaster was capable of taking off with an additional 33,100lb of fuel and bombs and it carried 64 per cent of the tonnage dropped by the RAF and RCAF during the war. In Britain 6,947 Lancasters were built and Victory Aircraft in Canada built 430 Lancasters. Of these, 3,932 were lost in action. Lancasters flew a total of 156,000 sorties and dropped 608,612 tons of bombs. Marshal of the RAF, Sir Arthur T. Harris, chief of Bomber Command, said that it was 'The finest bomber of the war! Its efficiency was almost incredible, both in performance and in the way it could be saddled with ever-increasing loads without breaking the camel's back.'

After the Dams Raid 617 Squadron resumed its elite role in July 1943 with attacks on Italian power stations and ports. 617 Squadron carried out highly specialised attacks, many of which employed the 12,000lb Tallboy and 22,000lb Grand Slam bombs. The Bouncing Bomb mine, weighing 9,250lb, and the Grand Slam, a 22,000lb

Wing Commander Guy Gibson VC. DSO* DFC*

7

The Dam Busters' insignia, showing a broken German dam as its centrepiece.

special-purpose bomb also designed by Barnes Wallis to penetrate concrete and explode below the surface to create an earthquake effect, could only be delivered by the Lancaster.

On 15 September 1943 a raid on the Dortmund-Ems canal proved particularly costly, with many of the Dams Raid survivors being shot down. Wing Commander Leonard Cheshire took command on 10 November and together with Squadron Leader Mick Martin, himself a brilliant exponent, developed the Squadron's low-level, precision marking and bombing techniques for attacks on defended targets. Cheshire controlled raids flying at low level in a Mosquito and later a Mustang. This role as a master bomber required skill, luck and great courage. In 1944 617 Squadron attacked factories, communications and railway marshalling yards, mainly in France (though a devastating raid, under intense anti-aircraft fire, was made against Munich on 24 April). A notable deception operation for D-Day was followed on 9 June by the first dropping of the Tallboy or 12,000lb earthquake bomb on the

One of the few remaining Lancasters is the Battle of Britain Memorial Flight's PA474, one of only two airworthy Lancasters out of 7,377 manufactured. Built in Chester in 1945, PA474 never saw active service although it had been destined for the Far East, until the dropping of the first atomic bombs and the capitulation of Japan saw PA474 assigned to photo reconnaissance duties in Africa instead.

Saumur railway tunnel, an important German supply route for Normandy, with great success. Further Tallboy operations brought destruction to U-boat pens, E-boat bases and V-weapons sites.

The 45,000-ton German battleship *Tirpitz*, moored in north Norwegian waters, was potentially a grave threat to allied shipping in the Atlantic or on the Russian convoy routes. All previous attempts to sink the ship had been unsuccessful. Plans to attack it with a smaller version of the bouncing bomb (codenamed *Highball*) in 1943 had come to nothing. On 15 September 1944 seventeen Lancasters of 617 Squadron led by Wing Commander Tait and ten of 9 Squadron attacked the *Tirpitz* from Yagodnik, a Russian airfield near Archangel, because Kaa Fjord, the target area, was too far from British airfields. Seventeen Tallboy bombs were dropped but the ship's protective smokescreen hid any resulting damage. However, the *Tirpitz* had been severely hit and was moved to Tromsö Fjord, just within range of RAF Lossiemouth where today 617 Squadron and its Tornado GR.4s are based. 617 and 9 Squadrons attacked on 29 October dropping thirty-two Tallboys but once more results were uncertain. Finally, on 12 November eighteen aircraft of 617 Squadron and ten of 9 Squadron found the *Tirpitz* with no cloud or smokescreen cover and no German fighter protection. Sustaining two direct hits, the ship was rent by an internal explosion and turned over.

617 Squadron flew its last operation on 25 April 1945 when it attacked Hitler's mountain retreat in the Alps at Berchtesgaden, Austria, with Tallboy bombs.

On 16 May 1983 617 Squadron commemorated the fortieth anniversary of the famous Dams Raid by entertaining the survivors of that epic operation. In a further tribute of the great raid the Tornadoes' individual aircraft identity letters painted on the fins were those carried by twelve of the aircraft flown by Wing Commander Guy Gibson's crews in May 1943.

Starring in two films, the *Guns of Navarone* and *Operation Crossbow*, like the Dam Buster Lancasters, The Battle of Britain Memorial Flight's PA474 served with the RAF with turrets removed while used as a reconnaissance aircraft. She appears throughout this book as the only example in Britain of a flying Lancaster.

# CHAPTER ONE

# Operation *Chastise*

Early in March 1943 several Lancaster aircrews in 5 Group Bomber Command were told that they were being posted forthwith to Scampton aerodrome, the 57 Squadron station a few miles north of Lincoln. They were to join Squadron 'X', which was being formed under the leadership of 24-year-old Wing Commander Guy Gibson DSO* DFC*. No other information was forthcoming. No one was told why they had been chosen and most were on their way within twenty-four hours. Gibson chose Squadron Leader Henry Melvin 'Dinghy' Young DFC*, who came from 57 Squadron, as his 'A' Flight Commander and Squadron Leader Henry Eric Maudslay DFC as his 'B' Flight Commander. He also recruited other fine pilots like Flight Lieutenant 'Mick' Martin DFC RAAF, probably the RAF's greatest exponent of low-level bombing, and Flying Officer Joseph Charles 'Joe' McCarthy, who had just completed his first tour, to join his new squadron. From Gibson's old squadron came Flight Lieutenant John Vere 'Hoppy' Hopgood DFC*. But not all the crews were 'hand-picked'. Many of them who arrived at Scampton on 30 March had completed fewer than ten operations and some had not yet flown one. By 24 April the number of crews was reduced to twenty-one. Gibson told them that the squadron had been formed to attack a particular target, the identity of which could not be revealed to anyone until briefing for the operation took place. Security would be at maximum and anyone caught talking about the squadron outside Scampton would be severely disciplined. We would be training for an unidentified period by night and at low level.

During the next six weeks there were few days when they were not flying. At first it was just low level at 200ft above the ground. As time wore on more and more flying was over water, the sea, rivers, or canals by day and then gradually by night. Tinted screens were affixed to the Perspex around the cockpit in the daytime to simulate night flying. Flight Lieutenant Les Munro RNZAF was one who had two close calls during training, which could well have had disastrous results. 'The first one was when flying down the North Sea at low level at night in rather hazy conditions when all of a sudden there appeared immediately ahead of us a convoy of ships. I quickly requested the wireless operator

### AVRO LANCASTER B.Mk I (Type 464 Provisioning)

| | |
|---|---|
| **Power Plant** | Four Rolls-Royce Merlin 28 12-cylinder Vee liquid-cooled engines rated at 1,460hp at 6,250ft in 'M' gear and 1,435hp at 11,000ft in 'S' gear. |
| **Performance** | Max speed: 271mph at 6,250ft and 281mph at 11,000ft. Time to climb: 20,000ft in 41.6 minutes. Service ceiling: 20,000ft (at maximum weight), 24,500ft (at mean weight). Range: (with standard fuel and 10,000lb bomb load) 1,040 miles. |
| **Dimensions** | Span: 102ft. Length: 68ft 10in. Height: 20ft 4in. Wing area: 1,300 sq. ft. |
| **Bomb Load** | One 9,250lb cylindrical airdropped 'Upkeep' mine. |
| **Armament** | Two .303in Browning machines guns in Frazer Nash FN5 hydraulically operated turret in nose, four .303in machine guns in FN20 rear turret. |

to fire off the colours of the day. In the light cast by the flares I could see a number of barrage balloons attached to the various ships by cables. I immediately pulled back on the control column and with the good fortune of 'Lady Luck' went shooting up through the balloons and cables and cleared the convoy without hitting either. The convoy remained silent with the ships giving off a ghost-like appearance.

'The second one was when flying across the Fen country southwest of the Wash. A seagull was a bit slow in avoiding the monster intruding over its habitat and hit the front screen to my left of dead centre, smashed a hole in the screen and came through the cockpit like a cannon ball between the flight engineer and myself. Hit the curtain shielding the navigator's compartment and ended up as a rather messy lump of flesh and feathers on the cockpit floor. Again luck was on my side! If it had hit the screen only a matter of about 18 inches to the left it would have hit my head and face with disastrous results. At the height at which I was flying, maybe one crashed aircraft and no survivors!'

Crews practiced flying over Derwent Water and attacking the dam with a newly designed bombsight. Judging the distance from the target proved equally simple, by making use of the twin towers, which flanked both the Möhne and Eder dams. A triangular wooden 'sight' was made with a peephole at the apex and nails at the other two ends. The bomb aimer would peer through the peephole and when the nails lined up with the towers, release his mine. They all laughed at the idea that they might be going to attack a dam. They all thought that the *Tirpitz* was the target. To achieve the optimum bombing altitude, two Aldis lamps fitted to the fuselage were played on to the water until they met in a figure of eight at precisely 60ft.

*Opposite:* Barnes Wallis, designer of the Upkeep bouncing bomb and the Tallboy and Grand Slam earthquake bombs.

Wing Commander Guy Gibson DSO* DFC* (centre), CO of 106 Squadron 14 March 1942-March 1943 with his two flight commanders, Squadron Leader John Searby (left) and Squadron Leader Peter Ward-Hunt DFC (right) at Syerston. Gibson, having completed two bomber tours and one night fighter tour, left to form 617 Squadron and Searby took over command of 106. Behind is Gibson's Lancaster III ED593 ZN-Y '*Admiral Prune II*' which survived at least seventy-two ops and finished the war as a ground instruction airframe. (IWM)

**617 Squadron, RAF Scampton, Lincolnshire. 5 Group, 16/17 May 1943.**
**Primary targets: Möhne, Eder and Sorpe dams. Secondary targets: Schwelm (Lister), Ennepe and Diemel dams.**

| Aircraft | Captain | Target | Remarks |
|---|---|---|---|
| ED932 *G-George* | Wing Commander Guy Gibson DSO DFC | Möhne/Eder | Released mine at Möhne |
| ED864 *B-Beer* | Flight Lieutenant David Astell DFC | Möhne | Shot down en route to the dam |
| ED887 *A-Apple* | Squadron Leader Melvyn 'Dinghy' Young DFC | Möhne | Hit Möhne Dam. Lost off Dutch coast on return. |
| ED906 *J-Johnny* | Flight Lieutenant David J.H. Maltby DFC | Möhne | Hit the Möhne Dam |
| ED925 *M-Mother* | Flight Lieutenant John V. 'Hoppy' Hopgood DFC* | Möhne | Lost at the Möhne Dam |
| ED929 *L-Love* | Flight Lieutenant Dave J. Shannon DFC RAAF | Möhne/Eder | Released mine at Eder |
| ED937 *Z-Zebra* | Squadron Leader Henry E. Maudslay DFC | Möhne/Eder | Lost after hit by blast of his own bomb |
| ED909 *P-Popsie* | Flight Lieutenant Mick Martin DFC RAAF | Möhne | Released mine at Möhne Dam |
| ED912 *N-Nuts* | Flight Lieutenant L.E.S. Knight RAAF | Möhne/Eder | Breached the Eder Dam |
| ED865 *S-Sugar* | Pilot Officer Lewis J. Burpee DFM RCAF | Sorpe | Lost on outward flight. |
| ED934 *K-King* | Flight Sergeant Vernon W. Byers RCAF | Sorpe | Lost on outward flight. |
| ED936 *H* | Pilot Officer Geoff Rice | Sorpe | Hit the sea before crossing enemy coast. Aborted. |
| ED921 *W-William* | Flight Lieutenant J. Les Munro RNZAF | Sorpe | Hit by flak on outward flight. Aborted |
| ED924 *Y-Yorker* | Flight Sergeant Cyril T. Anderson | Diemel/Sorpe | Did not bomb |
| ED927 *E-Edward* | Flight Lieutenant Robert N.G. Barlow DFC RAAF | Sorpe | Lost on outward flight. |
| ED918 *F-Freddy* | Flight Sergeant Ken W. Brown RCAF | Sorpe | Released mine at Dam wall |
| ED923 *T-Tommy* | Flight Lieutenant Joe C. McCarthy DFC RCAF | Sorpe | Released mine at Dam wall |
| ED886 *O-Orange* | Flight Sergeant W.C. Townsend | Ennepe | Released mine at Dam wall |
| ED910 *C-Charlie* | Pilot Officer Warner Ottley | Lister | Lost en route to the dam. |

Up until the day of the operation crews were kept in the dark about its real purpose. But imaginations raced when on 13 May Barnes Wallis' 'bouncing bombs' were delivered to Scampton. Rather than spheres, the mines were cylindrical and were made to spin in reverse before being dropped, so that they would skim over the tops of torpedo booms. To the crews the bomb looked like 'an outside garden roller'. They would be slung beneath the aircraft, the bomb doors having been removed and replaced by special fittings. Security at Scampton reached a high point over the next forty-eight hours. There was no chance of a trip into Lincoln. In the early afternoon of 15 May the Tannoy came to life: 'All pilots, navigators and bomb aimers of 617 Squadron report to the briefing-room immediately.' The great moment had arrived and nineteen crews were to spend the next four or five hours learning all about the Ruhr dams, listening to Wing Commander Gibson and to Barnes Wallis; the crews studied models of the dams as well as the route they were to follow. Every known concentration of anti-aircraft fire was noted as well as every possible landmark. No effort was spared to equip them for the 'op'. Then they were dismissed, with the injunction that they were to tell no one what the targets were. Preparations continued on the 16th and then all the aircrew were called for briefing. The Lancasters were to fly across the North Sea at 150ft, then across occupied Holland at 100ft and into Germany at 'nought feet'.

At about 3 o'clock on that balmy, sunny Sunday afternoon the teleprinters at Scampton chattered out the orders from Group. 'Code name for 5 Group Operation Order B.976 is *Chastise* ... Zero Hour: 22.48.'

The Lancasters took off in three waves. The first nine aircraft were to target the Möhne and then carry on to the Eder dam followed by other targets as directed by wireless from 5 Group Headquarters. The second wave of five was to act as a diversionary force and to attack the Sorpe, and the final five were detailed as back-up aircraft with alternative targets at Schwelm, Ennepe and Diemel dams if they were not needed in the main attacks. The first wave would fly in three sections of three aircraft about ten minutes apart.

Up until the day of the operation crews were kept in the dark about its real purpose. But imaginations raced when on 13 May Barnes Wallis' 'bouncing bombs' were delivered to Scampton. Rather than spheres, the mines were cylindrical and were made to spin in reverse before being dropped, so that they would skim over the tops of torpedo booms. To the crews the bomb looked like 'an outside garden roller'. They would be slung beneath the aircraft, the bomb doors having been removed and replaced by special fittings. Security at Scampton reached a high point over the next 48 hours. There was no chance of a trip into Lincoln. In the early afternoon of 15 May the Tannoy came to life: 'All pilots, navigators and bomb aimers of 617 Squadron report to the briefing-room immediately.' Les Munro recalls. 'The day of the Dams Raid had arrived and for the majority of the crews the first indication of the target was when entering the briefing room and viewing the tapes on the wall.' Nineteen crews spent the next four or five hours learning all about the Ruhr dams, listening to Wing Commander Gibson and to Barnes Wallis and studying models of the dams. Les Munro adds. 'The actual target did not give much cause for concern but the fact that the route to the targets led through the heavily defended area of the Ruhr did.' Every known concentration of anti-aircraft fire was noted as well as every possible landmark.

Pilot Officer Geoff Rice flew so low that his Lancaster hit the sea before crossing the enemy coast and he lost its bomb. Rice, a hosiery mechanic in peacetime who had maintained knitting machines in Hinckley, aborted and flew back on two engines. *W-William*, flown by Flight Lieutenant Les Munro RNZAF, part of the northern wave of aircraft with the Sorpe as their target, was also forced to abort, as he recalls. 'Our route was to fly due east across the North Sea and cross the Dutch coast at the coast of Vlieland. When flying down the Waddenzee side of the sand dunes of the coast my aircraft was hit by a single light shell, which severed the intercom and electrical systems. Without instrumentation at low level it was impossible to carry on and I made the decision to return to base with my Upkeep still on board.' 'Bill' Astell DFC flew into an obstruction and it ripped the mine off his Lancaster and killed them all.

The remaining Lancasters swung up the Rhine and arrived over the Ruhr and the first target, the Möhne Dam. As Gibson flew over a hill he saw the lake and then the dam itself. In the moonlight it looked 'squat and heavy and unconquerable ... grey and solid as though it were part of the countryside itself and just as unmoveable. We'd never practiced anything like it'

Gibson went in and sent his mine bouncing three times towards the concrete wall but it sank and exploded sending up a column of water. When the lake settled he saw that the dam had not been breached. The Upkeep mine had probably stopped and sunk just short of the dam, possibly having hit and broken the anti-torpedo nets thus clearing the way for the following mines. Flight Lieutenant Mick Martin DFC RAAF in *P-Popsie* watched the whole 'process'. 'The Wing Commander's load was placed just right and a spout of water went up 300ft into the air.'

The next two Lancasters missed. Brilliantly-coloured flak from guns in the sluice towers and lower dam wall hit *M-Mother* flown by Flight Lieutenant 'Hoppy' Hopgood. Tracers hit both port engines.

The bomb aimer released the mine a fraction of a second too late. Bouncing across the lake it leaped over the low parapet and exploded with a vivid yellow flash on the roof of the powerhouse on the other side of the dam. Hopgood clung grimly to the controls well aware that he could not gain more height for the crew to bale out. Hopgood banked the doomed Lancaster round to the right, away from the valley and said to his crew, 'For Christ's sake get out'. Only two men made it before the Lancaster exploded. Hopgood and the three other crew were killed when the Lancaster exploded and crashed about three miles beyond a village near the dam where it burst into flames and glowed fiercely throughout the rest of the attack.

*Opposite:* Flight Lieutenant David Shannon DFC RAAF and his crew in 106 Squadron shortly before joining the Dam Busters.

On 13 May the only fully armed live Upkeep mine to be spun and dropped before *Chastise* was released from a Lancaster in a trial five miles off the Kent coast at Broadstairs.

Next it was Mick Martin's turn. They caused a huge explosion up against the dam but still the dam held. The mine had probably hit the water slightly off level and thus did not bounce straight and it had veered off to the left and exploded near the southern shore of the lake. Gibson flew just ahead of Martin and to his right to distract the German defences and told his own gunners to fire back. *P-Popsie* was hit but not badly damaged. The fourth and fifth hits on the dam by 'Dinghy' Young and David Maltby finally breached the dam. Martin, who flew alongside Young to draw some of the flak, saw the first jet very clear in the moonlight and saw that the breach 'was about 50 yards wide.'

When Maltby attacked he saw the small breach in the centre made by Young's Lancaster and noticed that there was crumbling along the crown so he turned slightly to port but remained straight and level, and their mine was released. It bounced four times, struck the wall and 'sent up water and mud to a height of 1,000ft'.

Six minutes after Maltby's attack the breach was confirmed. In the end Young's breach in the centre and Maltby's to the left were joined together by the force of the escaping water to make a single breach 76m wide.

Gibson, who was now flying on the far side of the dam to distract the gunners, recalled '... we began to shout and scream and act like madmen over the R/T, for this was a tremendous sight, a sight which probably no man will ever see again. Quickly I told Hutch to tap out the message, 'Nigger' to my station and when this was handed to the Air Officer Commanding there was (I heard afterwards) great excitement in the operations room. The scientist jumped up and danced around the room.

'Then I looked again at the dam and at the water, while all around me the boys were doing the same. It was the most amazing sight. The whole valley was beginning to fill with fog from the steam of the gushing water. Down in the foggy valley we saw cars speeding along the roads in front of this great wave of water, which was chasing them and going faster than they could ever hope to go. I saw their headlights burning

Flight Sergeant Ken Brown RCAF and his crew of *F for Freddie* just prior to joining the Dam Busters.

Flying Officer Joseph Charles 'Big Joe' McCarthy DFC RCAF, a burly 23-year-old, 6ft 3in Irish-American from New York City, had just beaten the odds by completing his first tour with 97 Squadron at Woodhall Spa, on 11 March 1943. A few days later he received a telephone call from Guy Gibson. The 24-year-old wing commander told him, 'I'm forming a new squadron. I can't tell you much about it except to say that we may only be doing one trip. I'd like you and your crew to join us.' It was on 17 March that 'Squadron X' was formed, at Scampton in Lincolnshire. McCarthy, who was fascinated by all things aeronautical, was a favourite of his fellow pilots and was known on the squadrons as 'the big blonde American'. On his uniform he wore dual shoulder flashes 'USA' and 'Canada'. Born in St James, Long Island, on 31 August 1919, Joe McCarthy was raised in Brooklyn. His family had a summer home on Long Island where one of his summer jobs was as a lifeguard at Coney Island, the money helping to pay for private flying lessons at Roosevelt Field where, in 1927, Charles Lindbergh had taken off on his epic solo New York-to-Paris flight. In 1940-1941 McCarthy tried three times to join the US Army Air Corps but he never heard back from them!

and I saw water overtake them, wave by wave and then the colour of the headlights underneath the water changing from light blue to green, from green to dark purple, until there was no longer anything except the water bouncing down in great waves. The floods raced on, carrying with them as they went – viaducts, railways, bridges and everything that stood in their path. Three miles beyond the dam the remains of Hoppy's aircraft were still burning gently, a dull red glow on the ground. Hoppy had been avenged.'

Gibson and Maudslay and Flight Lieutenant's Dave Shannon DFC RAAF and Les Knight DSO RAAF flew on to the Dam Busters' next target, the Eder dam, the largest masonry dam in Germany. The Eder dam was not defended by guns but as Shannon said, 'The Eder was a bugger of a job' lying in very difficult terrain along a valley and very hard to find. Shannon only found the dam after Gibson fired a Very light over it. Gibson called Astell but there was no reply and then ordered Shannon to make his attack in *L-Love*. Shannon tried three times to get a 'spot-on' approach but was never satisfied. To get out of the valley after crossing the dam wall he had to put on full throttle and make a steep climbing turn to avoid a vast rock face. He described his exit with a 9,000lb bomb revolving at 500rpm as 'bloody hairy'. Then Gibson told him to take a 'breather' and *Z for Zebra* piloted by Squadron Leader Henry Maudslay DFC went in. He made two runs without releasing his mine and then Shannon made two more unsuccessful attempts before launching his weapon. It was way off centre. Then Maudslay made his run and his mine bounced over the dam wall and exploded in the valley below. Gibson called him up to ask him if he was all right and all he said was, 'I think so' and those were the last words that were heard from him. Badly damaged over the Möhne by the detonation of his own Upkeep weapon, Maudslay crashed near the German border between the Dutch village of Netterden and the German hamlet, Klein Netterden, 1¾ miles east of Emmerich, Germany. There were no survivors.

Finally, it was Knight's turn; the last of the main wave of nine aircraft. They did one dummy run and got it just about right. They circled and went in again at about 800ft. At 60ft the Lancaster levelled off and

Lancaster III ED817 of 617 Squadron, which was used to carry out drop tests of the 9,150lb Upkeep mine at Reculver before the weapon was finally cleared for use.

Lancaster III ED825 of 617 Squadron, which was used at A&AEE Boscombe Down for handling trials of the fully loaded bomber. This is the Lancaster that Flight Lieutenant Joe McCarthy used on the Dams Raid after his original aircraft went unserviceable and he made ten runs against the Sorpe before returning safely to Scampton. ED825 was lost with Flying Officer G.H. Weedon RCAF and crew on 10 December 1943. All were killed.

Guy Gibson's Lancaster III ED932/AJ-G showing the Upkeep mine mounted between the pair of side-swing callipers and the belt drive to the weapon. The belt drive was attached to the hydraulic motor in the forward end of the bomb bay by which means the mine was back-spun before release. The mine was filled with a high explosive called Torpex and fitted with a hydrostatic fuse.

617 Squadron flew a series of low-level training flights all over Britain where they practiced over lakes like the Derwent near Sheffield and the reservoirs at Uppingham (Eyebrook) near Corby (pictured) and Abberton near Colchester and Bala Lake in Wales.

21-year-old Squadron Leader Henry Eric Maudslay DFC who joined 617 Squadron from 50 Squadron. Originally from the Cotswold village of Broadway in Worcestershire, he was an accomplished middle-distance runner and former Captain of Boats at Eton.

Guy Gibson and his dog 'Nigger'.

Flight Lieutenant David J.H. Maltby DFC, born at Baldslow near Hastings in May 1920, had trained as a mining engineer before the war and he had joined the RAFVR in 1940, winning the DFC with 106 Squadron on Hampdens. He had flown a total of twenty-eight ops on Hampdens on 106 and Manchesters and Lancasters on 97 Squadron. Maltby's new crew, all sergeants, arrived at Woodhall Spa on 18 March prior to beginning his second tour. They were posted to 617 Squadron a week later. Three of them had yet to fly on operations.

seconds later they released their mine. A huge column of water was thrown up to about 1,000ft. Their mine had hit bang in the middle of the dam and had blown a hole straight through it. There was great excitement among Knight's crew and they were all on a high for a few minutes. Gibson called up and said, 'OK fellas, that's your job done. No hanging about, you know. Make your way home' Gibson described the breach 'as if a gigantic hand had pushed a hole through cardboard'. Banking below him, Les Knight reported a 'torrent of water causing a tidal wave almost 30ft high'. The crew of **N for Nan** watched in awe as car headlights in the path of the water turned from bright white to murky green to nothing. Melvin Young's nickname 'Dinghy' was transmitted back to 5 Group Headquarters to be received with yet more celebration.

The Lancasters flown by Flight Sergeant Ken Brown and Flight Lieutenant Joe McCarthy headed for the 226ft-high Sorpe dam. The Upkeep mine was only effective against concrete dams but as the Sorpe was an earth dam their instructions were to fly over and along the line of the dam at 60ft, releasing the bomb as near the centre of the dam as they could.

Arriving over the valley, McCarthy initiated a diving attack on the dam nestled at the bottom of two steep hills. Coming over the top of one hill, using full flaps to keep the speed of his 30-ton Lancaster under control, McCarthy dived down the slope toward the 765-yard long dam. To escape he had to apply full power to his four Packard-built Rolls-Royce Merlin's and climb at a steep angle up the side of the second hill. And if that wasn't difficult enough, a thick mist was filling the valley as he arrived. The blinding moonlight turned the mist into a writhing phosphorescent pall, which made it extremely difficult to judge the bomber's height above the lake. On the third attempt to locate the target, McCarthy almost flew **T For Tommy** into the water. It was not until the tenth run that bomb-aimer, Sergeant George 'Johnny' Johnson, was satisfied and released the bomb from a height of just 90ft. The weapon exploded squarely on top of the parapet, damaging and crumbling for more than 50 yards the crown of the earthen wall.

Flight Lieutenant Joe McCarthy's crew (AJ-T). From left to right: Sergeant G.L. Johnson, bomb aimer; Pilot Officer D.A. MacLean, navigator; Sergeant R. Batson, front gunner; Flight Lieutenant Joe McCarthy; Sergeant W.G. Radcliffe, engineer; and Sergeant L. Eaton, wireless operator. Missing from this photo is Flying Officer D. Rodger, the rear gunner.

Flight Lieutenant E.G. 'Bob' Hutchison and Wing Commander Guy Gibson DSO* DFC* shortly before boarding Lancaster *G-George* for the Dams Raid, 16/17 May 1943. On 106 Squadron Hutchison was Gibson's wireless operator on the night of 17/18 January 1943 when broadcaster Richard Dimbleby of the BBC flew aboard their Lancaster on the raid on Berlin. (IWM)

Shortly thereafter Flight Sergeant Ken Brown attacked the dam. His trip was quite eventful. Even before he reached the Sorpe his gunners shot up three trains en route. They were fired on by flak and hit in the fuselage but suffered no serious damage to the aircraft. They found the Sorpe dam with no trouble and could see it quite clearly at the northern end of the Sorpe river. The ground rose steeply on each side, heavily wooded, with a church steeple on our line of approach, all, except the river and dam, swathed in mist. The only good point appeared to be that there were no defences. After two or three abortive runs, Brown dropped flares along the approach route. They could see that the top of the dam was already damaged. Brown made ten runs on the Sorpe and finally dropped his mine on the eleventh run. The mine exploded on impact and caused a crumbling of 300ft the crest of the dam wall.

Squadron Leader Young's Lancaster was hit by flak at Castricum-aan-Zee, Holland, and crashed into the sea with the loss of all the crew. Flight Sergeant Townsend attacked the Ennepe dam but, like Brown, failed to breach it. Townsend was ordered to attack the Ennepe dam on the Schelme river. He made three runs on the dam before his bomb aimer, Sergeant Charles Franklin DFM, was satisfied. Their bomb was released, bounced once, and exploded 30 seconds after release. *O-Orange* made it safely back, landing at 6.15am. Most of the latter part of the homeward trip was flown in broad daylight.

The 'last resort' targets, the Lister (Schwelm) and Diemel dams were not attacked. However, the damage inflicted in the first two attacks proved the operation's success. The surge of water from the Möhne and Eder dams knocked out power stations and damaged factories and cut water, gas and electricity supplies. As many as 1,300 civilians, including about 500 Ukrainian women slave labourers died. Eight Lancasters were lost, fifty-three men were killed and three were captured. Pilot Officer W.H.T. Ottley's Lancaster was hit by flak near Hamm as they started to change their route when told to proceed to the Lister dam. Ablaze and with the outer port engine dead, Sergeant Fred Tees, the rear

*These pages:* The Möhne Dam the day after the raid on the Ruhr dams by Lancasters of 617 Squadron 16/17 May 1943. Nineteen Lancasters set out for the Ruhr dams but three were missing by the time that they arrived over the target. Wing Commander Guy Gibson went in and sent his mine successfully bouncing up to the concrete wall of the Möhne Dam, where it sank and exploded. The next two Lancasters missed – one of them being shot out of the sky but both the fourth and fifth hit and finally breached the dam. The Möhne reservoir contained almost 140 million tons of water and was the major source of supply for the industrial Ruhr twenty miles away.

*These pages:* Three Lancasters went on to bomb the Eder, sixty miles from the Ruhr, which was also breached. The Eder was even larger than the Möhne, containing 210 million tons of water. Eight of the Lancasters and fifty-six of the 133 men who flew on the raid failed to return. (René Millert via John Williams)

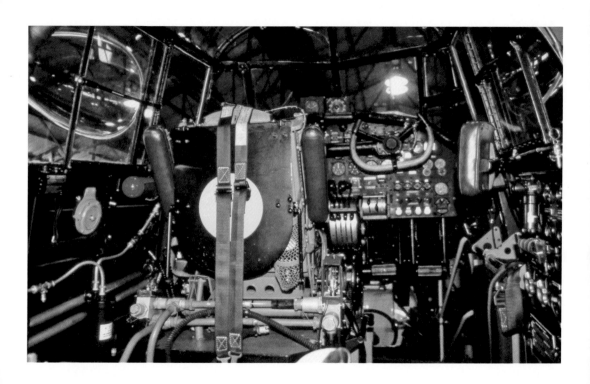

*Right:* A photo-reconaissance view of the Ruhr valley showing the effects of 300-plus million gallons of water on the industrial heartland of Germany.

*Opposite:* Debriefing of Guy Gibson's crew after their return from the 'Dams' raid. Air Chief Marshal Sir Arthur Harris and Ralph Cochrane look on as 617 Squadron's Intelligence officer Squadron Leader Townson sits down with Pilot Officer F. M. 'Spam' Spafford DFM, bomb aimer, Pilot Officer Terry H. Taerum, who was from Calgary, Canada, and Flight Lieutenant Richard Algernon D. Trevor-Roper DFM, rear gunner. Gibson is middle right, hidden by Trevor-Roper, who received the DFC for his part in the Dam's raid.

Wing Commander Guy Gibson VC DSO* DFC*.

Flight Lieutenant (later Squadron Leader) Harold 'Mick' Martin DSO DFC (left) flanked by the station CO, Group Captain J.N.H. 'Charles' Whitworth DSO DFC; HM King George VI and Guy Gibson (right). at Scampton on Thursday 27 May 1943. By the end of the war Martin, who was awarded the DSO for his part in the Dams raid and who received a bar to his DSO and DFC, was the only Australian airman to have won five British awards in the conflict. He was granted a permanent commission in 1945 and commanded 2nd TAF and RAF Germany from 1967 to 1970, retiring from the RAF in 1974 as Air Marshal Sir Harold Martin KCB DSO* DFC** AFC. He died on 3 November 1988.

Flight Sergeant Ken Brown RCAF is introduced to HM King George VI by Guy Gibson at Scampton on Thursday 27 May 1943.

Waiting to be received at Buckingham Palace on 22 June 1943. L-R: Flying Officer D.R. Walker; Pilot Officer George A. Deering RCAF; Sergeant H.J. Hewstone; Pilot Officer Torger Harlo Taerum RCAF; Sergeant Stefan Oanacia RCAF; Flight Sergeant Ken Brown RCAF; Sergeant H.B. Feneron; Flight Lieutenant Joe McCarthy DFC RCAF.

gunner with twenty-one operations to his credit, heard Ottley say apologetically, 'Sorry boys. I'm afraid we've bought it.' Their Lancaster crashed northeast of Dortmund and blew up. There was only one survivor.

The results of the operation were radioed to 5 Group Operations Room at Grantham where Air Chief Marshal Arthur 'Bomber' Harris, Barnes Wallis and others were waiting for news. On hearing the code word, Wallis, who until then had been morose, punched the air with both fists. Harris turned to him and said: 'Wallis, I didn't believe a word you said when you first came to see me. But now you could sell me a pink elephant!' Another story, probably apocryphal, was that Harris needed to ring Sir Charles Portal, Chief of the Air Staff, who was at that moment in Washington DC visiting President Roosevelt. The AOC picked up the telephone and said to the WAAF switchboard operator who controlled calls out of the 5 Group HQ, 'Get me the White House' 'Yes sir' replied the WAAF and put Harris through to the White House Hotel in Grantham, which was popular with 5 Group officers!

The euphoria at Grantham became more muted when news of the losses came in. Of the 133 men who flew on the raid, 56 failed to return. Wallis, who was troubled greatly by the losses, said, 'it was the most amazing feat the RAF ever had or ever could perform'. The massive Möhne, Eder and Sorpe dams served the industrial Ruhr Basin and more than a dozen hydroelectric power plants relied on their waters. So did foundries, steel works, chemical plants and other factories fuelling Germany's war effort. The War Cabinet noted with satisfaction the damage done to German war power.'

The raid received maximum publicity. Gibson was awarded the VC and many of the officers got DFCs and DSOs. Scampton was honoured by a visit from their majesties the King and Queen and the decorations were presented by the Queen, (the King being in Africa), at a special investiture on 22 June.

Twenty-two veterans of the Dams Raid were killed on ops. Guy Gibson was sent to America as an air attaché but he begged the Air Ministry to allow him to return to operations. At Woodhall Spa Gibson persuaded the CO of 627 Squadron to let him fly a Mosquito, against his better judgement, for the operation to Rheydt on the night of 19/20 September 1944 when he was to act as controller for the raid. He did not return. Over Walcheren both engines of Gibson's Mosquito cut and the aircraft crashed near the sea wall at Steenbergen, a small rural town in the southern Dutch province of North Brabant. Gibson and his navigator 23-year-old Squadron Leader James Brown Warwick DFC, an Irishman and veteran of two tours, were killed.

*Per Ardua Ad Astra*? Press on regardless? Gibson had ended his briefing for the Dams Raid by saying: 'Well chaps if you don't do it tonight you will be going back tomorrow night to finish it off.'

On 22 June 1943 after the Investiture at Buckingham Palace 617 Squadron celebrated. Left to right: Joe McCarthy, Les Munro, unknown American; Pilot Officer Fred M. 'Spam' Spafford, Gibson's bomb aimer; Guy Gibson; unknown American; Flight Lieutenant Dave Shannon; Flight Lieutenant 'Mick' Martin; Eve Gibson, Pilot Officer Toby B. Foxlee, Martin's front gunner; Flight Lieutenant Jack Leggo, Mick Martin's navigator; and Flight Lieutenant R.C. Bob Hay, Martin's bomb aimer.

*Right:* Repairs to the Möhne Dam after its breach.

*Opposite:* Flight Lieutenant Dave J. Shannon DSO DFC RAAF, Flight Lieutenant Algernon Trevor-Roper DFC DFM, Gibson' rear gunner, and Squadron Leader George Holden DSO DFC* MiD. Shannon was among those awarded the DSO for the Dam's raid. Holden who as CO of a Halifax squadron had flown on raids over the Alps to Italy took command of the Dam Busters' in July 1943.

# CHAPTER TWO
# After the Dams

After the euphoric Dams Raid 617 Squadron settled down to work again – not, as most expected, to the hammering of German cities and industries but to specialized targets which needed accurate bombing by a small force. In August 617 moved to Coningsby, nearby, where there were hard runways which Scampton lacked. Late in August it was noted that massive concrete sites for the launching of V-1 and V-2 weapons were springing up in Northern France, which would require accurate bombing with the biggest possible bombs. They would be 617 Squadron targets for the foreseeable future. 617, meanwhile, had moved again, this time to Woodhall Spa, near Coningsby, where they would be the only squadron. Accommodation was temporary at first and the nearby Petwood Hotel, taken over by the RAF, was their billet.

On 15/16 July 1943 617 Squadron carried out its first operation since the Dams Raid in May. Guy Gibson had been told that he had done enough operations and was not allowed to fly again, and Squadron Leader George Holden DSO DFC* MiD took command of the 'Dam Busters'. It had been decided to keep the Dam Busters in being as an 'old lags' squadron (Harris' affectionate and respectful name for experienced men who only wanted to fly ops) and to use it for independent precision raids on small targets. These would be carried out using the Stabilising Automatic Bomb Sight (SABS), which had been invented at Farnbrough in 1941 and incorporated a bulky gyro. In perfect conditions SABS could aim a bomb very accurately but a bomber using it had to run perfectly straight and level up to the target for ten miles. Harris said this would result in too many bomber losses but the argument was that SABS could be used economically by a small force operating at a fraction under 20,000ft over a well-marked target. At 5 Group the Air Officer Commanding (AOC), Air Vice Marshal The Honourable Sir Ralph A. Cochrane KBE CB AFC intended that 617 be trained to use SABS and deliver Barnes Wallis' new ten-ton bombs coming off the drawing board.

The targets on the night of 15/16 July were two power and transformer stations in Northern Italy. The intention was to disrupt the supply of electricity to the railways carrying German troops and supplies to the battle front in Sicily using twelve Lancasters of 617 Squadron and a dozen more from 5 Group. Because of the distance which was beyond the round trip range of the Lancaster, landfall would be made at Blida airfield in North Africa. Six of the Dam Busters were led by Holden to Aquata Scrivia, near Genoa, and the other six, to San Pola d'Enza, near Bologna, were led by Squadron Leader David Maltby DSO DFC. The raids were not successful. No flares or markers were carried and the targets were partially hidden by haze. Maltby reported that he had bombed on target and had seen blue flashes but one bomb and some of the incendiaries 'hung up' but they had successfully dropped these on the Genoa-Spezia railway line. There was little opposition and two Lancasters of the supporting force were lost. All the Dam Busters landed safely at Blida. Les Munro's Lancaster was damaged by shrapnel from his own bomb casing and damage was caused to the bomb aimer's panel and his starboard tyre burst, although he managed to land safely. After landing, Flight Lieutenant Joe McCarthy threw his parachute down digustedly and said, 'If we'd only carried flares we could've seen what we were doing.'

In North Africa bad weather grounded the Lancasters for ten days and they finally flew home on Saturday 24 July via Leghorn (Livorno) where bombs were dropped through the persistant haze into the harbour below. The bombing was uneventful, carried out on a time-and-distance run from Corsica. On 30 August 617 Squadron moved to Coningsby, about fifteen miles south of Lincoln, because it had a tarmac runway.

On the night of 15/16 September, exactly four months after the famous Ruhr dams raid, the Dam Busters were tasked to carry out a precision attack on the banks of the Dortmund-Ems canal at Ladbergen near Greven. The target was just south of the junction with the Mittelland canal where there was a raised section where aqueducts carry the canal over a river. This time the delayed-fuse mines were the new 12,000lb light-case bomb (not the 12,000lb Tallboy earthquake bomb developed later), which had been made in three sections bolted together with a six-finned tail unit on the end. It was so big that it needed special bomb trolleys to move it from the store and it took thirty-five minutes to be winched into the bomb bay of each Lancaster. The first attempt on the night of 14/15 September by eight Lancasters had been aborted. Squadron Leader David J.H. Maltby DSO DFC and crew, all of whom had flown on the Dams Raid, were lost on the way home eight miles north-east of Cromer when their Lancaster cart-wheeled into the North Sea.

*Opposite:* Bill Reid VC during a visit to an anti-aircraft battery. Acting Flight Lieutenant William 'Bill' Reid RAFVR and his crew of *O-Oboe* of 61 Squadron was awarded the VC for his actions on the operation to Düsseldorf in November when he bombed the target and got his Lancaster home after it as badly damaged by fighter attacks. Reid, the son of a Scottish blacksmith and not quite twenty-two years old was on his ten 'op'. Reid joined 617 Squadron after recovering from his ordeal. On 31 July 1943 Reid became a PoW when his Lancaster was brought down over France by a 1,000lb bomb dropped by an aircraft overhead during the bombing of both ends of a railway tunnel at Rilly-La-Montage, which was being used as a flying-bomb store. Reid and his WOp/AG were thrown clear when the nose of the Lancaster broke off as it spun down. He spent ten months in *Stalag Luft III* and *Stalag Luft IV*.

On 16/17 September 1943 eight Lancasters of 617 Squadron and four from 619 Squadron set out to bomb the Anthéor viaduct near Cannes on the coastal railway line leading to Italy. The Lancaster crews found the viaduct in the moonlight without trouble but their bombs missed the target. American bombers finally destroyed the viaduct.

With little sleep, eight of the crews were ordered back into the air the very next night, 15/16 September, to try again with the 12,000lb light-case bombs. The attack was led by Squadron Leader George Holden DSO DFC* MiD in *S-Sugar. Sugar's* crew included Flying Officer 'Spam' Spafford as bomb aimer and three other men who had flown with Gibson in the attack on the Möhne dam. Flight Lieutenant Mick Martin, who had returned from leave and had demanded to take Maltby's place piloted *P-Popsie.* Flight Lieutenant Dave Shannon piloted *L-Love,* No.2 in the second formation. Les Knight and *N-Nan* were No.3 in the first formation. Flying Officer Geoff Rice, who had aborted *Chastise* after hitting the sea on the

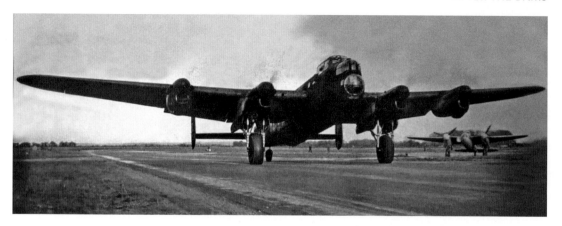

DV402/X taxies past one of the Mosquitoes used for target marking at Woodhall Spa.

outward flight, captained a fourth 'Dam Buster' crew. In the control tower at Coningsby Joe McCarthy, now a Squadron Leader with a DSO for the Dams Raid and a bar to his DFC added at the beginning of his third tour, watched as the eight Lancasters took off and headed east for the Dortmund-Ems canal at around midnight.

A wall of heavy fog lay along the frontier of Germany and Belgium as the aircraft flew in at rooftop level. It had moved in from the east 'without warning, almost without precedent.' Holden took them across the Dutch coast and over an industrial area with no shortage of anti-aircraft batteries. Bang, bang, bang and all of his fuel tanks were hit. There was a mile of burning fuel flying out behind him and he

dropped out of the sky. *S-Sugar* half-turned, dived and rolled to earth. It exploded on the ground in successive bursts as the oil tanks, then the bombs, exploded. Some said later that Flight Lieutenant Ralf A.P. Allsebrook DSO DFC, the deputy controller, should have called off the operation when the fog had moved in but they pressed on. Allsebrook is thought to have bombed eventually but where his bomb went is not known. They never found the wreckage of his Lancaster either. Flight Lieutenant Harold S. Wilson was heard briefly over the R/T saying something about going in to attack. The 12,000lb bomb was still aboard when his Lancaster hit the ground about 200 yards beyond the canal and it made a crater 200ft across. Pilot Officer William Divall was heard briefly over the R/T but that was the last anyone ever heard from him. Wilson and Divall had been prevented from flying the Dams Raid in May because of sickness in their crews.

Martin, Knight and Flying Officer Rice turned to avoid an airfield whose flare path could be seen below and eventually the three bombers went around north of Rheims. Knight's Lancaster was hit and he lost two engines. He received permission to jettison his six ton high explosive bomb load. About four minute's later N for Nan flew straight into a tree, caught fire and Knight was killed. Two of the crew were captured and four individually trekked across occupied Europe to Gibraltar. In December 1943 they burst into the Officers' Mess at Woodhall Spa wearing French berets.

Martin spent eighty-four minutes and Shannon forty-five minutes in the fog at low level over this heavily defended area in search of their target. Geoff Rice tried for an hour to find the canal. Finally, on the thirteenth run Flight Lieutenant R.C. 'Bob' Hay DFC* Martin's South Australian bomb aimer and the Squadron Bombing Leader since 617 Squadron's formation, got a glimpse of water in the swirling fog and they at last dropped the bomb. A little later they hurtled back across the canal and saw the water boiling where the bomb had exploded, a few feet from the bank, just a few feet too far, because the bank was still there. Shannon got a quick sight of the high banks of the canal. He wheeled the Lancaster along

Flying Officer Don Cheney's Tallboy bomb goes down over the unfinished V-2 rocket storage and launching site at Watten, France, on 19 June 1944 during the attack by two 617 Squadron Mosquitoes and nineteen Lancasters.

the water and his bomb aimer called, 'Bomb Gone!' There was an 11-second delay on the fuse so they only dimly saw the explosion. These three alone returned to Scampton. Martin and Shannon were awarded bars to their DFCs and Rice the DFC. Knight was later 'mentioned in dispatches'. Pilot Officer Rice and his crew, all of whom flew the dams raid, were shot down on the operation to the John Cockerill steel works at Liège on 20/21 December 1943. Rice was thrown clear as the Lancaster exploded in mid-air killing the rest of his crew. Despite a broken wrist, he evaded capture for six months until April 1944 by which time the Belgian Resistance had moved him to Brussels.

On 10 November 1943 Wing Commander Geoffrey Leonard Cheshire DSO** DFC took command of 617 Squadron. Les Munro recalls. 'Leonard quickly gained my respect both as a man and a leader. It was not long following his arrival that a renewed sense of purpose and reason for being developed

Flight Lieutenant Harold Wilson's crew of 617 Squadron were killed in action on 15/16 September 1943 in the disastrous attempt by 617 Squadron to breach the Dortmund-Ems canal. In May Wilson's crew had been due to fly the Dams Raid, but owing to illness they were scrubbed from the battle order at the last minute.

Flight Lieutenant Mick Martin DSO DFC.

in the squadron. In conjunction with Micky Martin, Cheshire introduced low-level marking of targets by the squadron with the result that 617 became highly efficient in destroying individual targets. The cosmopolitan make-up the squadron was exemplified when it was restructured into three flights with Cheshire an Englishman as CO and three originals, McCarthy an American, Shannon an Australian and myself a New Zealander, as flight commanders. It later became known as the Cheshire era and I have always felt a great deal of satisfaction and pride in being part of that period.'

On the night of 8/9 February 1944 Cheshire led a dozen of his Lancasters to bomb the Gnome & Rhône aero-engine factory at Limoges 200 miles southwest of Paris. The factory was undefended except for two machine guns and Cheshire made three low-level runs in bright moonlight to warn the 300 French girls working the night shift to escape. On the fourth run he dropped a load of 30lb incendiaries from between 50 and 100ft. Each of the other eleven Lancasters then dropped a 12,000lb bomb with great accuracy. Ten of the bombs hit the factory and an eleventh

The Gnome-Rhône aero engine factory at Gennevilliers, near Paris, before the raid by a dozen Lancasters of 617 Dam Busters Squadron on 8/9 February 1944. (IWM)

Photo-reconnaissance taken after the attack on the Gnome-Rhône aero engine factory Wing Commander Leonard Cheshire DSO* DFC, the Dam Busters' new CO (who had completed four operational tours of duty) made three low-level runs on the factory in bright moonlight to warn the French factory workers to escape. On his fourth run he dropped 140 30lb incendiaries from between 50 feet and 100 feet and each of the other eleven Lancasters dropped a 12,000lb bomb with great accuracy. Ten bombs hit the factory and the remaining one fell in the river alongside. The factory was severely damaged and production almost completely ceased. There were few if any French casualties and all the Lancasters returned safely. (IWM)

Since the beginning of 1944 617 Squadron, now commanded by Wing Commander Geoffrey Leonard Cheshire DSO** DFC*, had successfully employed the tactic of marking and destroying small industrial targets at night using flares dropped by a Lancaster in a shallow dive at low level. Cheshire, who was on his fourth tour, was born in 1917 at Chester and was educated at Stowe and Merton College, Oxford, where he was a member of the University Air Squadron between 1937 and the outbreak of war. At 25 he was the youngest group captain in the RAF and he had dropped back to wing commander so that he could resume bomber operations. Five years earlier he received an Honours degree in Law at Oxford and at 24, on leave in New York, he had met and married 41-year-old Constance Binney, who had been America's top movie star. In England Cheshire liked a suite at the Ritz on leave and to bask in The Mayfair cocktail bar.

A Tallboy being hoisted aloft. By the end of the war 854 of these fearsome weapons, which were filled with approximately 5,760lb of Torpex D high explosive had been dropped on a variety of targets ranging from shipping, U-boat and E-boat pens to viaducts, canals and V-weapon sites.

fell in the river alongside. The AOC Air Marshal the Hon. Ralph Cochrane was quick to appreciate that if a single aircraft could mark a target accurately for a squadron then it should be possible for a squadron of properly trained crews to mark targets with similar accuracy for the whole group. The Lancaster was vulnerable to light flak at low level and a more manoeuvrable aircraft was required for the operations Cochrane had in mind. Cheshire was aware of the limitations of the Lancaster and he had already decided that the best aircraft for low-level marking. He briefed the AOC on his ideas and Cochrane allocated 617 Squadron a Mosquito.

On the night of the 16/17 December 1943 RAF heavy bombers and Oboe Mosquitoes were despatched to bomb two V-1 flying-bomb sites near Abbeville in northern France. At Flixecourt the nine Lancasters of 617 Squadron dropped their

On 31 May/1 June 1944 eighty-two Lancasters and four Mosquitoes of 5 Group attacked and destroyed a railway junction at Saumur, 125 miles north of the battle area in France without loss. On 8/9 June the first 12,000lb Tallboy bombs were used on this night by 617 Squadron in a raid on a railway tunnel near Saumur. The raid was conceived in great haste because a Panzer unit was expected to move by train through the tunnel. The target was illuminated with flares by four Lancasters of 83 Squadron and marked at low level by three Mosquitoes. Twenty-five Lancasters of 617 Squadron then dropped their Tallboys with great accuracy. The huge bombs exploded under the ground to create miniature 'earthquakes'. One actually pierced the roof of the tunnel and brought down a huge quantity of rock and soil. The tunnel was blocked for a considerable period and the Panzer unit was badly delayed. No aircraft were lost from the raid.

SAUMUR TUNNEL. RECONSTRUCTION REP No. K S 1476

73

12,000lb Tallboy bombs accurately on the Green TIs and LB TIs but the markers were 350 yards from the V-1 site and none of the Lancasters' bombs were more than 100 yards from the markers. Five more raids on V-bomb construction sites were flown during the rest of the month. On 30/31 December a further attempt was also made to mark a V-l flying bomb site at Cherbourg that had been missed on earlier raid. Unfortunately, the markers were placed 200 yards from the target. All the bombs dropped by the ten Lancasters of 617 Squadron, though well grouped, missed the site completely.

In January 1944 Mick Martin was awarded a bar to his DSO. Mick Martin was made up to squadron leader and given temporary command of the squadron. On 12/13 February in an attack by eight Lancasters of 617 Squadron (and four from 619 Squadron) with 12,000lb blockbusters on the Anthéor viaduct, near Cannes, when running in to attack at under 200ft through heavy fire, Martin's Lancaster was hit repeatedly. 'Bob' Hay was killed and the engineer wounded. The bomb release was destroyed and the controls badly damaged. Martin succeeded in flying the crippled Lanc back through severe electrical storms to Cagliari in Sardinia, where he made an excellent landing in difficult circumstances. The sides of the valley were very steep and the viaduct was defended by guns which damaged both Martin's and Cheshire's low-level aircraft. Martin was awarded a second bar to his DFC in November 1944 after he had completed two tours on heavy bombers and one as a Mosquito Intruder pilot. By the end of the war he was the only Australian airman to have won five British awards in the conflict.

The Dam Busters would later return to the viaduct with even bigger bombs but this first raid simply alerted the Germans to the vulnerability of the structure and soon after the flak batteries moved in. One Lancaster of 619 Squadron was lost when it came down in the sea off Portugal while trying to reach Gibraltar. The Dam Busters now began retraining as a specialist high-altitude bombing squadron to drop ten-ton bombs on suitable enemy targets. Crews believed, wrongly as it turned out, that their immediate target might be the *Tirpitz*, which was not bombed by 617 until almost exactly a year later.

The Dam Busters' first Mosquito sortie was on 5/6 April when the seemingly fearless Cheshire and his chunky little navigator Flying Officer Pat Kelly marked an aircraft factory at Toulouse on his third pass with two red spot flares from a height of 800-1,000ft. Cheshire used this aircraft on 10/11 April to mark a signals depot at St Cyr during a dive from 5,000 to 1,000ft. These successes led to 617 Squadron receiving four Mosquitoes for marking purposes and this resulted in 5 Group – the Independent Air Force, as it was known in Bomber Command – receiving its own PFF force. Nos 83 and 97 Lancaster Squadrons rejoined 5 Group, as backers-up and 617 Squadron and 627 Mosquito Squadrons were redeployed from Coningsby and Oakington respectively to Woodhall Spa. While the Dam Busters 'lorded it' in Petwood House, 627 were relegated to a batch of Nissen huts on the far side of the airfield!

In the station cinema at Coningsby, Cochrane and Cheshire addressed the assembled Lancaster crews of 83 and 97 PFF Squadrons and Mosquito men of 627 Squadron as to their new role. Cochrane opened the meeting by saying that 617 Squadron had made a number of successful attacks on important pinpoint targets and it was now intended to repeat these on a wider scale. The Lancaster pathfinder squadrons were to identify the target areas on H2S and were to lay a carpet of flares over a given target, under which 627 Squadron would locate and mark the precise aiming point. 5 Group Lancaster bombers would then destroy the target. Cheshire, a tall, thin and imposing figure, took the stand in front of the assembled crews who all knew of his legendary reputation in the RAF and he explained carefully how the low-level marking business was done. What the Lancasters had to do was lay a concentrated carpet of hooded flares, the light from which would he directed downwards onto the target, making it as bright as day. The small force of Mosquitoes would orbit, find the aiming point and then mark it in a shallow dive with 500lb spot-fires. Marker Leader would assess the position of the spot-fires in relation to the aiming point and would pass this information to a 'Master of Ceremonies' in one of the pathfinder Lancasters. The MC would then take over and direct the Main Force Lancasters in their attack on the target.

A number of the raids that were now taking place were in preparation for the invasion of France by the Allied forces. The invasion required destruction of the French railway system leading to the landing area. The best method of doing this was by employing heavy bombers, but grave doubts existed at the highest level as to the accuracy with which this could he done. Winston Churchill was adamant that French lives must not be lost needlessly. On the night of 18/19 April, 202 Lancasters of 5 Group led by Leonard Cheshire carried out a mass attack on Juvisy marshalling yard in the Paris area after the target was marked at each end with red spot-fires by four Mosquitoes of 627 Squadron. Few French lives were lost, all but one Lancaster returned safely and the railway yards were so badly damaged that they were not brought back into service until 1947.

The real test of the new tactics had still to be made – against targets in Germany. 5 Group was therefore unleashed against three of these targets in quick succession – Brunswick on 22/23 April, Munich two nights later and Schweinfurt on 26/27 April. At Brunswick the initial marking by 617 Squadron Mosquitoes was accurate but many of the main force of Lancasters did not bomb these, partly because of a thin layer of cloud which hampered visibility, and partly because of faulty communications between the various bomber controllers. Sir Arthur Harris had sanctioned the release of the Mosquitoes to 617 Squadron and insisted they could be retained only if Munich was hit heavily. Cheshire's contribution to the success of the Munich operation on 24/25 April, when he led four Mosquitoes of the Marking Force in 5 Group, was mentioned in his VC citation on 8 September 1944. In part it said, 'Cheshire's cold and calculated acceptance of risks is exemplified by his conduct in an attack on Munich in April 1944. This was an experimental attack to test out the new method of target marking at low level against a heavily defended target situated deep in enemy territory. He was obliged to follow, in bad weather,

a direct route, which took him over the defences of Augsburg and thereafter he was continuously under fire. As he reached the target, flares were being released by our high-flying aircraft and he was illuminated from above and below. All guns within range opened fire on him. Diving [from 12,000 to 3,000ft and then flying repeatedly over the city at little more than 700ft] he dropped his markers with great precision and began to climb away. So blinding were the searchlights that he almost lost control. He then flew over the city at 1,000ft to assess the accuracy of his work and direct other aircraft. His own was badly hit by shell fragments but he continued to fly over the target area until he was satisfied that he had done all in his power to ensure success ... for a full twelve minutes after leaving the target area he was under withering fire, but he came safely though ... What he did in the Munich operation was typical of the careful planning, brilliant execution and contempt for danger which has established for Wing Commander Cheshire a reputation second to none in Bomber Command'. The crews who took part were: Cheshire and Pat Kelly; Squadron Leader Dave Shannon DSO and Len Sumpter; Flight Lieutenants Terry Kearns and Hone Barclay and Flight Lieutenants Gerry Fawke and Tom Bennett. Shannon, who was deputy master bomber and deputy leader, dived from 15,000 to 4,000ft but his markers hung up, while the fourth Mosquito got four spot flares away. Shannon received a bar to his DSO in September 1944 after he had completed many more important operational sorties with 617 Squadron. So far as Brunswick and Munich were concerned, considerable damage was done. In the case of Munich, 90 per cent of the bombs fell in the right place, doing more damage in one night that had been achieved by Bomber Command and the 8th Air Force in the preceding four years.

After these attacks, 5 Group turned exclusively to support the bombing campaign against interdiction targets in France in support of Operation *Overlord* and the D-Day landings. On 3 May, 346 Lancaster crews, two Oboe-equipped Mosquitoes and four Pathfinder Mosquitoes of 617 Squadron were briefed for the raid on Mailly-le-Camp, a pre-war French Army tank depot near Epernay east of Paris. Crews were told that it was a Panzer depot and training centre reported to house up to 10,000 Wehrmacht troops. British Intelligence had received word that the Panzer division was due to move out the next day so it had to be attacked that night. Individual bombing height was to be 7,100ft and the target was to be marked by Cheshire in a Mosquito. 5 Group was the first wave of 163 Lancasters and was to attack the southeast part of the camp while 153 bombers of 1 Group made up the second wave. Cheshire was the 'Marker Leader' in one of the four PFF Mosquitoes of 617 Squadron. Marking began at 2358 hours.

Petwood House Hotel at Woodhall Spa, the wartime mess for 617 *Dam Busters* Squadron. (Author)

Zero hour was 0005. 87 and 93 PFF Squadrons had already dropped flares and these lit up the area so that Cheshire, dropping to 1,500ft from 3,000ft, had no problem in locating his two red spot flares on target. Cheshire was not happy with their position and called up Squadron Leader Dave Shannon in the accompanying Mosquito to mark the site that needed to be bombed more accurately, dropping his red spot fires accurately at 0006 hours. Cheshire told the Master Bomber to hold the main attack off until he was satisfied. After Shannon had dived down to 600ft to lay the markers, Cheshire gave the master bomber the go ahead. Although the target was marked accurately and Cheshire passed the order to the 'Main Force Controller' to send in the Main Force, who were orbiting at a holding pattern to the north, and bomb. Wing Commander L.C. Deane of 83 Squadron instructed the wireless operator to give the 'Start Bombing' order but the message was distorted. In some cases the VHF radio frequency was drowned out by an American Armed Forces Network broadcast. Some men thought that the Germans were trying to jam their communications. Only a few Lancaster crews picked up the garbled message and went in and bombed. So too did a handful of other aircraft flown by experienced captains who realized that delaying dropping their bombs and circling the yellow datum point that had been laid near the village of Germinon could be disastrous. Deane knew that the delay in starting bombing by the Main Force was serious and he tried to send the message by Morse but it failed to transmit. Cheshire also tried to get through but he was unable to do so either. He then tried to abort the raid but this failed. The first wave did not receive instructions and began to orbit the target and the German night-fighters moved in and began to shoot down the Lancasters. Finally, the order to bomb was given, but forty-two Lancasters were lost. Fourteen were from 5 Group and twenty-eight from 1 Group. 5 Group had 'stirred the hornet's nest' and 1 Group 'had taken the stings.'

# CHAPTER 3
# D-Day to VE Day

Overhead on 5/6 June 1944, massive aerial support was given before dawn to the Normandy landings as over 1,000 aircraft including 551 Lancasters bombed coastal batteries at ten strong points along the fringes of *Gold, Juno* and *Sword* landing beaches. RAF Bomber Command flew 1,211 sorties. Operations *Taxable* and *Glimmer,* both devised by Wing Commander E.I. Dickie, created 'Phantom Fleets' on enemy radar screens. *Taxable* involved sixteen Lancasters of 617 Squadron and was a joint RN/RAF operation aimed at making the Germans believe that an invasion force was attacking the French coast between Dieppe and Cap d'Antifer. Attacks on enemy radar installations had all but destroyed their effectiveness, but care had been taken to leave enough operational to allow the Germans to deceive themselves that their radars were showing an invasion fleet.

On 8/9 June, 483 aircraft attacked rail targets at Alençon, Fougères, Mayenne, Pontabault and Rennes to prevent German reinforcements from the south reaching the Normandy battle area. Three Lancasters and a Mosquito failed to return. That same night the first 12,000lb Tallboy bombs developed by Barnes Wallis were used when twenty-five Lancasters of 617 Squadron dropped these fearsome weapons on the a railway tunnel near Saumur to prevent a Panzer unit moving up to the Normandy front by train. The target area was illuminated with flares by four Lancasters of 83 Squadron and marked at low level

by three Mosquitoes. The Tallboys were dropped with great accuracy and the tunnel was destroyed in a 'miniature earthquake'.

On 14 June, 221 Lancasters and thirteen Mosquitoes carried out a daylight raid on E-boats at Le Havre. Included in the force were twenty-two Lancasters of 617 Squadron, each loaded with a 12,000lb Tallboy bomb. Harris was still reluctant to risk his heavy bombers on daylight operations but Spitfires escorted both waves of the attack and only one Lancaster was lost. On 24 June, sixteen Lancasters and two Mosquitoes of 617 Squadron bombed the flying-bomb site at Wizernes with Tallboy bombs, the Dam Busters losing one Lancaster. Next day Wing Commander Leonard Cheshire, who always tried to increase bombing accuracy, accompanied seventeen Lancasters and two Mosquitoes to the Siracourt flying-bomb store in a P-51 with the purpose of using it as a low-level marker aircraft. The Mustang had only arrived that same afternoon and this was Cheshire's first flight in it! His Lancasters scored three direct hits on the concrete store with Tallboy bombs and Cheshire landed safely back at Woodhall Spa. (Cheshire would fly his hundredth op on 8 July and he was withdrawn from operations)

*Opposite:* A low-level photograph taken after the attack on Wizernes V-2 rocket site under construction in Northern France on 17 July 1944 by sixteen Lancasters of 617 Squadron with a Mosquito and a Mustang as marker aircraft. The 'Dam Busters' aimed 12,000lb Tallboy earthquake bombs with 11-second delay on the huge concrete dome, 20ft thick, which lay on the edge of a chalk quarry protecting rocket stores and launching tunnels that led out of the face of the quarry pointing towards London. One *Tallboy* that apparently burst at the side of the dome exploded beneath it, knocking it askew. Another caused part of the chalk cliff to collapse, undermining the dome, with part of the resulting landslide also blocking four tunnel entrances, including the two that were intended for the erected V-2s. Though the construction was not hit, the surrounding area was so badly 'churned up' that it was unapproachable and the bunker jeopardized from underneath. The site was abandoned and the V-2s were pulled back to The Hague in Holland where in September the Germans began firing them from mobile launchers. (IWM)

On 4 July, the Lancasters of 5 Group were given a special target, a flying bomb site at St-Leu-d'Esserent in the Pas de Calais, which was to be hit first by seventeen Lancasters of 617 Squadron supported by Cheshire in a Mustang and Flight Lieutenant Gerry Fawke in a Mosquito. St-Leu-d'Esserent consisted of an area of large caves tunnelled out some years before the war and used by the French to grow mushrooms. The Germans cleaned up the inside of the caves and used them to store V-1 flying bombs. The aim of the attack was to collapse the roof of the caves, which had been estimated to be about 25ft thick. A subsidiary aim of the raid was to devastate the road and rail communications running between the caves and the river. At the briefing crews were warned that the area was heavily defended by flak units and to keep a sharp lookout for night fighters. This was an all-5 Group bombing operation with a few 8 Group Pathfinders. Nine and 617 Squadrons carried the big 12,000lb Tallboy bombs while the rest of the Lancaster force carried about the same weight of bombs

Squadron Leader James Brown Warwick DFC who on 19/20 September 1944 was KIA with Gibson flying a Mosquito.

made up of 1,000lb and 500lb HEs. Many of the bombs were fitted with six-hour delay pistols. The target was bombed accurately and without loss.

Les Munro adds. 'It was only a month after D-Day that Cheshire, Shannon, McCarthy and I were taken off operations and so ended my operational career and my service on 617 Squadron. I have always maintained that the international and cosmopolitan make up of 617 was one of its strengths with its English majority strongly supported by men from the Commonwealth – Canada, Australia, Rhodesia and New Zealand and even two from the USA. In post-war years that cosmopolitan make up resulted in a strong worldwide association with all members fiercely loyal to 617 Squadron's history and their ties thereto.'

On 11 September, thirty-eight Lancasters of 9 and 617 Squadrons, accompanied by a PR.XVI Mosquito to provide up-to-date target information and weather report, flew to their forward base at Yagodnik on an island in the

A 12,000lb Tallboy bomb being loaded into Lancaster B.I ED763 KC-Z *Honor* of 617 Squadron at Woodhall Spa. This aircraft was flown by Flight Lieutenant Stuart Anning on the third raid against the *Tirpitz* on 12 November 1944.

Dvina River near Archangel, in northern Russia. One Lancaster returned en route and six others fell victim to bad weather and crash-landed in the Soviet Union. On 15 September, the attack, by twenty-eight Lancasters, twenty of which were carrying Tallboys and six or seven others twelve 500lb 'Johnny Walker' oscillating mines, went ahead and considerable damage was caused to the battleship *Tirpitz*. Subsequent photo-reconnaissance revealed that although badly damaged, the *Tirpitz* was still afloat (albeit beyond practical repair, although this was not known at the time.

On 24 September, listeners tuning in to their wireless sets for the news heard the announcer say that last night Lancasters of Bomber Command had carried out a successful attack on the Dortmund-Ems canal near Ladbergen, just north of Münster. Most of the damage to the canal, whose aiming point was the twin aqueducts over the River Grane where the level of the water was higher than the surrounding land, was caused by two direct hits by 12,000lb Tallboy bombs dropped by 617 Squadron at the opening of the raid. The other Lancasters carried 14,000lb of HE in their bomb bays and 1,500 gallons of petrol to get them to their target.

During October-December 1944 fifteen out of twenty raids on the Ruhr were in daylight. On 7 October, resuming its original role, 617 Squadron breached the Kembs barrage on the Rhine to prevent the Germans controlling the river flow during the Allied crossing. When the *Tirpitz* moved westward for repairs in a German dockyard it was attacked once more on 29 October but again the bomber crews could obtain only an oblique view of her through cloud. Some thirty-seven Lancasters (eighteen Lancasters each from 9 and 617 Squadrons plus a photographic aircraft from 463 Squadron) took off from Lossiemouth and attacked the *Tirpitz* in Tromsö Fjord. Thirty-two Lancasters dropped Tallboy bombs on estimated position of the capital ship. Though no direct hits were achieved, a Tallboy near-miss by the stern caused considerable damage, distorting the propeller shaft and rudder, which flooded the bilges over a 100ft length of the ship's port side. The damage meant that the *Tirpitz* was no longer

On 14 March 1945 thirty-two Lancasters and one Mosquito of 5 Group with four Oboe Mosquitoes of 8 Group attacked the Bielefeld and Arnsberg railway viaducts in Germany. Twenty-eight Lancasters dropped 12,000lb Tallboy bombs and the 617 Squadron Lancaster of Squadron Leader C.C. Calder dropped the first 22,000lb Grand Slam bomb, at Bielefeld. The Arnsberg viaduct, 9 Squadron's target, was later found to be undamaged but near misses at Bielefeld created an earthquake effect which caused 100 yards of the viaduct to collapse, as this photo by a Lockheed F-5 Lightning of the US 8th Air Force shows.

On 21 March 1945 the Arbergen railway bridge over the River Weser was attacked by twenty Lancasters of 617 Squadron who dropped 'Ten Ton Bombs' on the structure and damaged two piers of the bridge. One Lancaster was lost. In the photograph is Lancaster Mk.I Special PB996/YZ-C minus nose or dorsal turret, flown by Squadron Leader C.C. Calder.

Photographed on 22 March 1945, the battleship *Tirpitz* capsized in Tromsö Fiord by a 14,000lb *Tallboy* dropped during the raid by Lancasters on 29 October 1944. The hull is covered by snow and there is a hole in the starboard side.

able to steam under her own power. The *Tirpitz* was no longer seaworthy but the War Cabinet decided that the battleship must be sunk.

On Sunday morning, 12 November, Lancasters at last sent the *Tirpitz* to the bottom in Tromsö Fjord. It was the third attack made on the 45,000-ton battleship by Bomber Command with 12,000lb bombs, but this was the first time the attackers were able to see the ship properly. The weather was clear and there was no smokescreen. The *Tirpitz* was first sighted when the attacking force of thirty Lancasters of 9 and 617 Squadrons led by 26-year-old Welsh Wing Commander James B. 'Willy' Tait DSO*** DFC* was about twenty miles away. One 12,000-pounder apparently hit the *Tirpitz* amidships, another in the bows and a third towards the stern, and there were also two very near misses which must themselves have done serious underwater damage. The vessel was lying on its side, half submerged, with her red hull gleaming in the sunlight. At least two Tallboys hit the ship, which capsized to remain bottom upwards. The crew of the *Tirpitz* had been reduced from a complement of 2,000 to about 1,600, most of whom were engine room personnel, after the second attack. Around 900 men were killed, drowned or suffocated, having been trapped on board in watertight compartments. Only eighty-seven sailors were recovered from the ship by cutting through the double bottom from the outside.

The early months of 1945 saw a tremendous increase in Bomber Command's operations, both in tempo and number, forty raids being mounted in February alone. That same month, 617 Squadron, with Group Captain Fauquier now in command, was expanded from two flights to three with one carrying Tallboys and the others Barnes Wallis's 22,000lb Grand Slam bomb, the RAF's largest of the war. Known as 'Cookies' by RAF crews, the 4,000lb, 8,000lb and 12,000lb blast bombs were dubbed 'Block Busters' by Fleet Street. Grand Slam bombs could reach a velocity of 1,000 feet per second (680mph) when dropped from 20,000 feet. (Forty-one Grand Slam bombs were delivered before the end of the war in Europe).

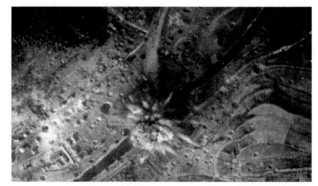

*These pages:* Three sequential views of a Grand Slam bomb being dropped from Lancaster PB996/YZ-C and the effects one of these earthquake bombs had on exploding. PB996 was struck off charge in November 1947 and is shown here in early night-bomber camouflague.

In the last months of the war 617 Squadron continued its support of the advancing Allied armies in north-west Europe by attacks on canals, viaducts, bridges, coastal defences, U-boat installations and the German navy. The bombing of former *U-boat* pens at Farge on the River Weser north of Bremen. The huge structure had a concrete roof 23ft thick. It had almost been ready for use when on 27 March 1945 twenty Lancasters of 617 Squadron attacked it and penetrated the roof with two 22,000lb 'Grand Slam'

Lancasters *en route* over the Alps to Berchtesgaden on 25 April 1945. Hitler's home, referred to as the 'Chalet' by the RAF, was the target for 359 Lancaster heavy bombers and 14 Oboe Mosquito and 24 Lancaster marker aircraft. Included in the mighty force were 33 Lancasters of 9 Squadron and 617, the Dam Busters, each carrying a 12,000lb Tallboy bomb.

Berchtesgaden from 18,000ft on 25 April 1945. Those who bombed the 'Chalet' mostly missed. A mountain peak between the Oboe ground station and the aircraft had blocked out the bomb release signal. Since Oboe signals went line of sight and did not follow the curvature of the earth, the further the target, the higher one needed to be and the Oboe Mosquitoes flew at 36,000ft because of the Alps. Crews heard the first two dots of the release signal and then nothing more. They were unable to drop and brought the markers back.

bombs, which brought down thousands of tons of concrete rubble and rendered the shelter unusable. It was thought that a target like this could probably withstand a 22,000lb bomb but whether it could withstand repeated hits could only be determined by experiments after the war.

On 9 April, forty Lancasters carried out the last raid on Hamburg when they raided oil-storage tanks and seventeen aircraft of 617 Squadron blasted the U-boat shelters in the already devastated city with 22,000lb Grand Slam and 12,000lb Tallboy bombs.

The end came on 25 April with a raid by 482 aircraft on coastal batteries on the Friesian Island of Wangerooge and in a fitting climax to bomber operations, on Hitler's mountain retreat at Berchtesgarden in the southeast corner of Germany. Hitler's home, referred to as the 'Chalet' by the RAF, was the target for 359 Lancaster heavy bombers and fourteen Oboe Mosquito and twenty-four Lancaster marker aircraft. Included in the mighty force were thirty-three Lancasters of 9 Squadron and 617 the 'Dam Busters', each carrying a potentially devastating 12,000lb Tallboy bomb in the bomb bay. At least 126 Mustangs of 11 Group RAF and ninety-eight P-51s from two American fighter groups provided escort relays along the route, a round trip of 1,400 miles. Those who bombed the 'Chalet' mostly missed (A mountain peak between the Oboe ground station and the aircraft had blocked out the bomb release signal. Since Oboe signals went line of sight and did not follow the curvature of the earth, the further the target, the higher one needed to be and the Oboe Mosquitoes flew at 36,000ft because of the Alps. Crews heard the first two dots of the release signal and then nothing more. They were unable to drop and brought the markers back) but the Berghof sustained much blast damage as a result of the bombs and the Tallboys. At the SS barracks, one building and several others were damaged. Bomber Command's last bombing operations were flown that night. Four days later Operation *Manna* began, as the Lancaster squadrons began dropping food and not bombs.

# CHAPTER 4

# 'A New Flight of Fancy?'
# Dam Busters Fact & Fiction

Think of a classic war film and then try and better the original – impossible. Hollywood tried unsuccessfully with *Memphis Belle* and countless others. An epic has to appeal to American audiences; i.e. it has to generate big bucks. One other reason for a remake is to improve on the original and/or introduce the subject to younger audiences. In 2006 Peter Jackson, of *Lord Of The Rings* and *King Kong* fame, announced that he would remake the 1954 British film classic *The Dam Busters* as *'The Dambusters'*. Jackson admitted that he 'really loved' the film as a child. He said. 'There's that wonderful mentality of the British during the war – that heads-down, persevering, keep-on-plugging-away mentality which is the spirit of Dam Busters'.

British matinee idol Richard Todd played superbly Wing Commander Guy Penrose Gibson DSO* DFC*, the leader of the daring operation and Michael Redgrave was equally as good as Barnes Wallis. Geoff Mayer in his Guide to British Cinema (Greenwood Press 2003) says that Todd claimed that *The Dam Busters* was the best military war picture ever made' and that 'the box office receipts in 1955 provided support' for his 'assertion'. The film was rightly nominated for Best British Film and Best Film from Any Source at the 1956 BAFTA Awards. Mayer adds: *'The Dam Busters* is a sturdy example of the popular cycle of mid-1950s films that looked back to World War Two as a means to celebrate British military achievements and sacrifices during that period. The film consists of two interconnected sections.

The first part details the obstacles faced by English design engineer Barnes Wallis in 1942 to produce a 'bouncing bomb' that would destroy German dams in the Ruhr heartland. The second half of the film necessarily shifts the emphasis away from Wallis to Gibson and his men as they practice low-level flying, followed by the prolonged climax as the planes cross enemy territory to reach the Ruhr.'

The last scene in the film, which involves Wallis and Gibson when the crew losses are known, is very poignant. Gibson says that he 'has letters to write'. Todd was not just acting out his lines. During the war Todd had had to write 'a lot of letters' to bereaved relatives of soldiers under his command. On the eve of D-Day, 6 June 1944, Todd was a 23-year-old First Lieutenant in the 7th Light Infantry Battalion, 5th Parachute Brigade. Of 610 men dropped, by the morning of D-Day only 240 were left.'

So, could anyone possibly improve on director Michael Anderson's original? It could be digitally remade in colour instead of the original black and white 'wet' film, which was chosen to give the 1954 film a documentary feel (just as *The Longest Day* had done). Considering the *The Dam Busters'* vintage, the special effects used were in the main superb but the enormous explosion as the Möhne dam is finally breached

A *Picturegoer* series postcard of Richard Todd as Guy Gibson, in *The Dam Busters*.

Shades of the Dam Busters. PA474 passes over Abberton reservoir south-south-east of Colchester, Essex. '... S.A.S.O. (Senior Air Staff Officer) has given permission for us to use the reservoirs at Uppingham and Colchester to practise on. He has fixed up with a film studio or something to rig up a special framework on the water barrage which will make them look very like our own objectives. From now on we are going to carry out attacks against these places using nine aircraft at a time. These attacks will begin tonight. The sort of thing I visualize is three flights of three aircraft flying in formation at night along our special route. We will reach the first lake; we will then attack singly, according to my instructions on the R/T from exactly 60 feet and at exactly 232 miles an hour ... In the meantime, other crews are to keep their hands in with bombing a spotlight flying over the Wash. Six other special crews will be sent to another lake to carry out a special form of attack there.' *Enemy Coast Ahead* by Guy Gibson VC DSO* DFC*.

Richard Todd and 'Nigger' on the set of *The Dam Busters* at Elstree in 1954.

was 'matted' on to the long shot of the dam by a contact special effects company in London's Soho. Now, their attempt looks about as realistic as bath water flowing vertically and it is visually unappealing, as are the model Lancasters shown crashing on fire. Computer Generated Imaging (CGI) would undoubtedly remove these irritating blips, which spoil the final few reels.

CGI could also be used to remedy the sight of the bulbous pumpkins beneath the Lancs with authentic-looking 'bouncing bombs'. In 1954 much of the 'Dam Busters' operation was still secret and Associated British were not allowed to show the actual bouncing bomb design. Jackson uses this to qualify his reasons for wanting to remake *Dam Busters* – or *Dambusters* as he called it.

CGI may replicate or fill in for dramatic flying sequences but will never adequately replace the wonderful flying in such epics as *The Blue Max* or TV's *A Piece of Cake* where triplanes and a Spitfire, respectively, are flown

Born in Ireland in 1919, Richard Todd spent part of his childhood in India with his father who was an army physician. Following his training at the Italia Conta School in the late 1930s, he appeared in productions at the Dundee Repertory Company prior to the Second World War, where he returned after military service during the war. In 1948 Todd won the part of Corporal Lachlan 'Lachie' MacLachlan, the prickly Scot who learns that he is dying, in *The Hasty Heart* starring Ronald Reagan and Patricia Neal. His role earned Todd a nomination for Best Actor at the 1950 Academy Awards and he won the Most Promising Newcomer Award at the Golden Globes. Todd's impressive film career includes such epics such as *Yangtse Incident* (1956) and *The Longest Day* (1962). *Yangtse Incident* was the second Anderson-directed war film, also based on a true incident, with Todd commanding HMS *Amethyst*, which was trapped by Chinese communists on the Yangtse River in 1949. In *The Longest Day* Todd requested and was given the part of Major John Howard, a British glider infantry officer who was Todd's commanding officer in 1944. In the 1960s and 1970s the theatre occupied much of Todd's acting career.

Just some of the crew and actors in front of one of the stars of *The Dam Busters.*

under bridges by ace 'stunt' pilots. CGI must surely save a film company vast expense on aircraft and pilots, though computer-generated Lancasters used as 'stand ins' for the real thing would hardly be appealing to the purists, especially when there are two Lancs in flying condition. CGI also removes the possibility of putting at least one non-flying Lanc, a Mosquito and a Wellington back into flying condition. In 1969 *The Battle of Britain* resulted in several previously redundant Spitfires and Hurricanes being returned to flying condition.

One big advantage of filming *The Dam Busters,* which began on location shooting in April 1954 at 617 Squadron's wartime station at Scampton was the availability of four flyable RAF Lancaster Mk.7s and pilots to fly them. All four Lancs were taken out of storage at 20 Maintenance Unit (MU), RAF Aston Down, and specially modified for the film. Three of these Lancasters had 'starred' in *Appointment In London,* Philip Leacock's feature film about a wartime Lancaster squadron starring Dirk Bogarde, which was premiered in 1953. For *The Dam Busters* the Lancasters were joined 'on set' by a Vickers Varsity on loan from the Bomber Command Bombing School, Lindholme, a PR.35 Mosquito and even a Vickers Wellington T.10, all of which were made available to Associated British for aerial filming. The Varsity was used as the camera aircraft. Michael Anderson

Robert Shaw (left) and Richard Todd during filming for *The Dam Busters.*

*WREN* cartoon of the stars of the film and Dam Buster pilots, *c.* 1955.

and his producer had selected the right people for the aerial filming and then let them get on with it without interference. German-born cinematographer Erwin Hillier, who had moved to England before the war, was appointed Director of Photography and he was also in charge of the aerial photography. Associated British's second unit team, led by Special Effects Photographer Gilbert Taylor, filmed much of the aerial footage from the Varsity. Some of the head-on shots of the Lancasters used in the film were taken from the rear turret of the Wellington. Hillier and Taylor used American Mitchell-type and Arriflex cameras.

The whole ensemble was brought together for filming sequences at RAF stations at Hemswell and Scampton, which were wartime Lancaster stations and in the 1950s were still in the front-line

defence of the UK, as Avro Lincoln and English Electric Canberra jet bomber stations. Scampton was home to four Canberra squadrons. It ensured that engineering support was available *in situ* although for spare parts it was necessary for the Lancs to be flown to 22 MU at RAF Silloth in Cumbria. The Air Ministry charged Associated British £100 per engine hour running time. Taking into consideration the number of aircraft and engines used, it worked out at up to £1,600 per hour,

Ready for take-off!

A poster for the greatest film of 1954.

not an insignificant sum of money in the 1950s. Today the figures translate to £1,620 per engine hour or £6,480 per Lancaster per hour. The total bill for the use of four Lancasters and their crews would be around £1.5 million at today's prices. The RAF put Scampton at the disposal of Associated British as its base for the main shooting. They were unable to secure permission to film the raid sequences over the actual Ruhr dams themselves, so much use was made of studio models and the Derwent Dam in the Derbyshire Peak District for filming. The Derwent reservoir was one of three lakes used by 617 Squadron in April and May 1943 for intensive flying training before the raid. Abberton reservoir near Colchester, which gave the crews a good idea of the calm waters of the Eder reservoir, and Uppingham (now Rutland Water) were also used.

April 1954 was a busy month for the Lancaster crews with familiarisation flights followed by the first filming sorties. May was less busy and the months of June and July were relatively unproductive where it concerned aerial filming involving the Lancasters. The second unit aerial filming was undertaken at Hemswell, Scampton, Kirton-in-Lindsey, Syerston, and Silloth throughout the summer. Scenes showing early tests of the bouncing bomb at Reculver were shot off the shoreline at Skegness in Lincolnshire because it was near to the main filming activity at Hemswell and Scampton. Scenes recreating the actual training flights in England and Wales and the operations over the Ruhr dams were filmed over and along Lake Windermere and Derwent Water and the dam where low-level formation runs were made by day and by night. And the bombers were flown between the twin towers of the Derwent Dam. August and September each saw close to twenty hours of air-to-air film work. For additional low-level filming in the Lake District, the Lancasters and second unit crew were detached to RAF Silloth in Cumbria at the end of August for a week, while the most intensive activity took place on 4 September, when RAF pilots and crews demonstrated their low level formation flying expertise during almost six hours of low-level formation flying over Lake Windermere. Sometimes the Lancs were flown at

very low level in a three-ship formation through the Kirkstone Pass in the Lake District towards Lake Windermere. When the Lancasters returned to Scampton roaring over the airfield in V-formation Todd noticed that 'there wasn't a dry eye in the house.'

Richard Todd also pays tribute to the flying skill of the RAF pilots when he said, 'Those RAF chaps took a lot of chances and did a wonderful, wonderful job for us.' After one filming sortie one of the crews returned with bits of branches and leaves attached underneath the aircraft, as they had evidently brushed a tree. The bombing runs on the Ruhr dams were flown at 60ft but the rushes showed that during filming 60ft actually looked much higher so for the low-level runs the crews were asked to fly at 40ft!

The flight to the dams over the Dutch lowlands was simulated over the dead flat fenlands between Boston in Lincolnshire and Kings Lynn, just across the Great Ouse in Norfolk. Scenes of the Lancasters crossing the 'enemy coast' were shot over Gibraltar Point near Skegness, or along the coast near Southwold in Suffolk or the west coast of Anglesey in North Wales. The scenes of inundation in the Ruhr Valley that appear towards the end of the film were photographed in 1954 when the area of the dams itself fell victim to a natural flood disaster. Michael Anderson sent a film unit to Germany specially to capture this event for incorporation in the final version of the film.

Location work was completed in September 1954. The film took about ten months from start of model shooting to seeing the first print from the lab. At Elstree the set builders and model makers re-created office interiors for Bomber Harris, Guy Gibson and Barnes Wallis.

The special effects used in the film are at best brilliant and at worse, very cumbersome and a little dated. The special effects boffins had to simulate explosions of the bouncing bombs and the dam walls crumbing under the massive back-pressure of water caused by the explosions of the aerial mines. Three enormous authentic scale mock-ups of the dams, their lakes and surrounding countryside were created at Elstree Studios. They measured 300ft long by 150ft wide, filled an entire sound stage and were filmed

Paul Brickhill, author of *The Dam Busters*.

by a camera mounted on a crane. Each model was lit for night and to simulate the appearance of water on a real lake, twenty-eight giant fans, each adjusted to a different speed, were positioned around the set to cause ripples on the surface of the water. The contact special effects company who 'matted' the enormous explosion as the Möhne dam is finally breached also added the tracer bullets and flak. To create the single close-up shot of Gibson in flight over the Möhne, looking out the left-hand side of the cockpit window of his Lancaster, it was necessary to shoot six separate 'travelling matts'. These were a studio shot of Todd in the mock up Lancaster cockpit, the model of the dam, photographed flak, the landscape background to the model dam, an explosion (featuring a different model) and a Lancaster in flight. Each matt had to be photographed at precisely the right angle of vision and each had to be in correct proportion to its size when viewed from that distance.

Jackson promised that his version, in production with a budget of £16-21 million, would be 'as authentic and as close to the spirit of the original as possible'. In 1954 no sequences were removed from the finished film, which was nominated for Best British Screenplay. R.C. Sherriff's tightly-scripted original screenplay was arrived at by paying homage to *Enemy Coast Ahead* by Guy Gibson and *The Dam Busters* by Paul Brickhill. Stephen Fry was hired by Jackson to pen a new script. Websites were awash – one might say flooded – with quips and snipes from worried film buffs, aviation enthusiasts and concerned moviegoers. According to Lester Haines, 'When Jackson first enquired about the film rights in the 1990s he was told that Mel Gibson had a plan to direct and possibly act in his own remake. [It is impossible now to imagine anyone filling the roles of Gibson and Barnes Wallis that Todd and Michael Redgrave (later Sir Michael) made their own]. Mercifully for cinemagoers that never happened. The result would almost certainly have been a *U-571*-style adaptation showing the Americans breaching the Möhne and Eder dams, in the process drowning an English army led by a sneering Alan Rickman on its way to massacre Scottish Highlanders.'

So, do we want a remake in colour with a revisionist plot and simulated Lancasters and a new score? (The *Dam Busters March* is as popular today as it was when it made the Top Ten in 1955 and remained there for more than a year. Eric Coates, the composer, died in 1957).

I say, take the original, retain 'The Dam Busters March', re-master it all in stereo, keep the models of the dams but use CGI to create the proper bouncing bombs and replace that irritating water spout when the Möhne is breached!

End of story, roll the credits!

## The Dam Busters – Separating Facts from Fiction

Reasons for the attacks

Operation *Chastise* involved nineteen Lancasters of 617 Squadron who took off from Scampton to breach the Ruhr dams with 'bouncing bombs' (code-named Upkeep) invented by Dr Barnes Wallis. It was, as Wallis said, 'the most amazing feat the RAF ever had or ever could perform'. The massive Möhne, Eder or Sorpe dams served the industrial Ruhr Basin and more than a dozen hydroelectric power plants relied on their waters. So did foundries, steel works, chemical plants and other factories fuelling Germany's war effort.

**Guy Penrose Gibson**

The 24-year-old wing commander had flown two bomber tours and one night-fighter tour at the time of the Dams Raid and had shot down four enemy aircraft at night. He had been awarded two DSOs and two DFCs.

**The crews**

Ages ranged from twenty to thirty-two. Of the 133 men who would crew the Lancasters on the secret operation only twenty of them were decorated. Gibson selected many of these, but in the main the crews were not decorated and some of them had not flown a tour. They came from all over the world: Australia, Canada, New Zealand and Great Britain. American pilot, Joe McCarthy from Brooklyn, had been a lifeguard at Coney Island.

**The raids**

Six dams were targeted. Apart from the Möhne, Eder and Sorpe dams shown in the film, secondary targets were the Lister (Schwelm), Ennepe and Diemel dams. The Möhne dam was 850 yards long and 140ft thick holding back 140 million tons of water in the lake twelve miles long. The Eder dam, the largest masonry dam in Germany was 1,310ft wide, 138ft high, 119ft thick at the base and 20ft thick at the top.

**Success or Glorious Failure?**

Eight Lancasters were lost; fifty-three men killed, three captured. As many as 1,300 civilians, including about 500 Ukrainian women slave labourers died. But the operation *was* a success. The raids forced the *Nazis* to rebuild and

Three Lancasters pass Lincoln Cathedral, during filming for *The Dam Busters*. Inside the cathedral are a series of stained glass windows commemorating the men of Bomber Command who lost their lives in the Second World War.

*Opposite:* Lancaster *City of Lincoln* threads its way along Derwent Water and over the dam on 19 May 1993 to celebrate the fiftieth anniversary of the Dams Raid. In the run up to the raid 617 Squadron practised flying over Derwent Water and attacking the dam with a newly designed bombsight. The Derwent reservoir was one of three lakes used by 617 Squadron in April and May 1943 for intensive flying training before the raid.

*Above left and right:* Squadron Leader Joe McCarthy DSO DFC RCAF and Squadron Leader Les Munro CNZM DSO QSO DFC JP at the Derwent Dam on 19 May 1993. (Author)

fortify the dams and in the process divert 10,000 war workers it could ill-afford to move from other tasks. *Luftwaffe* aircraft also had to be brought in from other areas to strengthen the defences in the Ruhr dams region. As for the effect on German morale; it was nothing short of catastrophic. The late Joe McCarthy, who made no less than ten bomb runs before releasing his mine, said that he would have risked his neck to drop barrels of butter on the dams if asked. The surge of water from the Möhne and Eder dams knocked out power stations, damaged factories and cut water, gas and electricity supplies. The Sorpe dam, though badly damaged was not breached but the Germans, unsure of dam's integrity, were forced to drain off over 50 per cent of the reservoir's capacity until the structure could be inspected and repaired.

*Chastise* proved that the war in Europe was being prosecuted dramatically well at a time most of President Roosevelt's advisers were committed to targeting Japan first. Winston Churchill used the raid as a coup to seek greater support from the USA. Two days after the operation, Churchill was given a standing ovation at the *Trident* Conference with Roosevelt in Washington.

## The Film

Only Formation 1 (nine Lancasters in three waves) from the three formations that were sent on the operation is featured in the film. The second formation, like the third formation, did not attack in waves but acted as a diversionary force to attack the Sorpe. The third formation of five crews brought up the rear and was used to fill in gaps left in the first two formations). All the model shots were filmed in the first three months of 1954. The twin Aldis lights beneath each Lancaster whose beams converged to form a 'figure 8' on the lake surfaces when the bomber was at exactly 60ft over the water did not result from a visit Gibson and his crews made to a London show but were developed by the 'backroom boffins'.

*Z-Zebra* (Maudslay) shown exploding just after the run on the Eder actually went down after the attack near the Dutch border.

In the US version in the 1950s 'Nigger', Gibson's black Labrador became 'Trigger', to avoid any racial problems.

The author
Paul Brickhill's *The Great Escape* is published in 1951. Brickhill, an Australian Spitfire pilot who was incarcerated in *Stalag Luft III* and Conrad Norton had written *Escape to Danger* (published in 1946). *The Dam Busters* was published late in 1951 and by Christmas had sold 50,000 copies in Britain alone. Another Brickhill best-seller was *Reach for the Sky,* the story of legless fighter ace, Douglas Bader, in 1954.

16 May 1955
First showing of *The Dam Busters*, on the twelfth anniversary of the raid, at the Empire, Leicester Square, London, in the presence of Princess Margaret. Also present, some of the surviving members of the dams raid that included Mick Martin, Harold Hobday, navigator AJ-N and Bert Foxlee, front gunner AJ-P, as well as Gibson's father and his widow, Eve.

20 May 1955
Film is specially shown at RAF Scampton station cinema.

5 September 1955
Film put on general release. Running time: 2 hours.

# Bibliography

*Barnes Wallis' Bombs: Tallboy, Dambuster & Grand Slam* Stephen Flower (Tempus 2004).

*Breaking The Dams: The Story of Dambuster David Maltby & His Crew* Charles Foster (Pen & Sword 2008)

*Dambuster – A Life of Guy Gibson VC* Susan Ottaway (Pen & Sword)

*Dambusters: The Definitive History of 617 Squadron At War 1943-1945* Chris Ward, Andy Lee, Andreas Wachtel (Red Kite 2008)

*Enemy Coast Ahead* Wing Commander Guy Gibson VC DSO* DFC* (Michael Joseph 1946)

*Filming The Dambusters* Jonathan Falconer (Sutton, 2005)

*Flying For Freedom: Life and Death in Bomber Command* Tony Redding (Cerebus 2005).

*Legend of the Lancasters,* Martin W. Bowman (Pen & Sword 2009)

*Living With Heroes: The Dam Busters* Harry Humphries (The Erskine Press 2003)

*The Battle of Britain Memorial Flight,* Martin W. Bowman (Airlife 2000)

*The Dam Busters* Paul Brickhill (Evans Bros. London 1951).

*The Dam Busters: Breaking the Great Dams of Western Germany 16-17 May 1943* Jonathan Falconer (Sutton 2003)

*The Dambuster Who Cracked the Dam: The Story of Melvin 'Dinghy' Young* Arthur G. Thorning (Pen & Sword 2008)

*The Dambusters* John Sweetman, David Coward & Gary Johnstone (Time Warner 2003)

*The Dams Raid Through the Lens* Helmuth Euler (*After the Battle*, 2001)

*We Will Remember Them: Guy Gibson and the Dam Busters* Jan van den Driesschen with Eve Gibson (Erskine Press 2004)